the breakup book

the breakup book

by monica sheehan

WARNER BOOKS

A Time Warner Company

Warner Books, Inc., 1271 Avenue of the Americas, New York, NY 10020
Visit our Web site at http://warnerbooks.com

Printed in the United States of America
First Printing: February 1999
10 9 8 7 6 5 4 3 2 1

 A Time Warner Company

Library of Congress Cataloging-in-Publication Data

Sheehan, Monica.
    The breakup book / Monica Sheehan.
        p.   cm.
    ISBN 0-446-67485-0
    1. Separation (Psychology)—Humor. 2. Man-woman
relationships—Humor. I. Title.
    PN6231.S495 S53 1999
    306.89'02'07—dc21   98-37517
                                                              CIP

Cover art design and text illustrations by Monica Sheehan

for my big sister nora
and for kate hartson,
thank you both
from the bottom of my heart
for all your help.

-m.

acknowledgments

I'd also like to thank my support system, my other sisters
mary jane, ann, and sarah, my sister-in-law margaret,
jon kleiman, kenny, liam, my favorite bartenders
stephen and rob,
everyone at the dub, and last but not least,
my best friend lynne.

with a special thanks to gerry, for
proofreading, making coffee and answering
my endless questions: 'does it work?'...
'is it funny?'... 'how do you spell that?'...
'tell me the truth, but is it funny?...'
merci.

-m.

the first...

28
days

get drunk.*

1

numbing yourself
is a common
response to losing
the relationship.

day

*if drinking is not an option go on to day 2.

eat whatever you want.

2

day

you are still in shock. put away the alchohol and move on to mallomars.

call in sick.

(tell them you have food poisoning.)

stay in bed
all day and
watch the
home shopping
network.

day 3

sad song disease kicks in.

4

day

you actually start relating to gloria estefan and the carpenters.

seek guidance.

5

start reading
your horoscope
(and his) in
every magazine
and paper you
can get your
hands on.

day

day

6

drive by his house

(more than once).

fear!!!

7

day

you will never
have another
relationship,
ever!!

loss of **8** concentration.

day

decision-making becomes difficult.

decaf or
regular?
lemon or
lime??
cup or
cone???

day **9**

start calling

day 10

just to hear
his voice
on the
answering
machine.

you cannot believe you
have stooped to this level.

11

denial sets in.

he will definitely
call today. sit by
the phone while
looking through
old photographs.

he will definitely not call!!

day 12

rip up old photographs and get rid of all memorabilia except his jean jacket.*

*it looks great on you and it's faded to perfection.

anger!
(he hasn't called.)

day 13

get a
haircut.
if you can't
change your
life, change
your hair.

give into temptation.

14

call him up at midnight to ask if you can borrow his reversible drill.

day

bargaining.

day 15

"so what
if he needed
his old
girlfriends."

self-improvement.

day 16

diet, self-help books, jane fonda and eight glasses of spring water a day.

day

17

revenge plans
start to develop.

go shopping.

day 18

if you're going
to be upset
you might as
well do it in
a new outfit
(or two).

revenge plans
don't
work out.

day 19

day

20

help!

start draining your friends with 2-hour play-by-play conversations about your hopeless relationship.

day

21

call your mother
for sympathy.

mistake.

22

get professional
help.

go to your
local psychic.

day

23

start broadcasting

how much **better** you feel; that you're happily single; and that it's definitely definitely **over!**

"it can't be definitely over!"

24

day

begin fantasizing about how much he needs you. you're the only one who really understands him. give it time and he'll come crawling back.

keep fantasizing.

25

rent some videos while you're waiting for him to crawl back.

day

come to
the brilliant
conclusion

26

that he's
too afraid
to make the
first move...

so you have
to do it for him.

go back to his old haunt.

day 27

get hit like a mack truck that you're a done deal. somebody else has filled your combat boots. aaaughh!!!

wake up **28** day depressed

and tired of the
pathetic patterns
in your life.
but then
you realize...

there's a

big world

out there...

with beautiful

art...

great music...

and true friends...

and the only
person
you really
have to
live with is
yourself.

so be comfortable
with you.

take a deep breath...

and move on.

p.s. you're better off.